Higher

and Other Poems of Faith

Steven Manchester

To Stephanie –
keep the Faith!

[signature]
2021

lbp

Luna Bella Press

Copyright © 2020 by Steven Manchester

Book Design by Barbara Aronica-Buck
Cover Art by Keith Conforti

Print ISBN-13: 978-0-9841842-9-3

Visit our website at www.LunaBellaPress.com

First Luna Bella Press Printing: April 2020

Printed in The United States of America

For those who need to know they're not alone

Acknowledgments

First and forever, Jesus Christ—my Lord and Savior. With Him, all things are possible.

Paula, my beautiful wife, for loving me and being the amazing woman she is.

My children—Evan, Jacob, Isabella and Carissa—for inspiring me.

Mom, Dad, Billy, Julie, Caroline, Caleb, Randy, Kathy, Philip, the Baker girls, Darlene, Jeremy, Baker, Aurora, Jen, Jason, Jack, Lucas, the DeSousa's, Laura—my beloved family and foundation on which I stand.

Countless friends—Brian Fox, Claude Tetreault, Mark Rodrigues, Rob Letendre, George Cournoyer, and many more—who have walked beside me on my spiritual journey.

Contents

Higher

A pair of wide-eyes search the unfamiliar playground,
as the giggle of captivating innocence turns to a squeal.
Seated upon a swing, a young boy looks back, begging,
"Push me higher, Daddy!"
With only a few pumps of his legs and a set of strong
but gentle hands behind him, his fears are conquered
and he steps into the sky.

A pair of eager legs march into adolescence,
tripping on the discovery that the world can be unkind.
Again, looking back, those same eyes betray his silent plea,
"Push me higher, Dad."
The labored hands of love take his desperate grip
and lead him on his chosen path.
Still, the sky is within reach.

A pair of old, tired arms long for a hug that has died,
as two feeble legs buckle at the knees.
With weary eyes, he looks toward heaven and whispers,
"Push me higher, Father."
A pair of stronger, more loving hands lift him up
and carry him home.
For eternity, that sky shall be his carpet.

Forgotten Guide

I've climbed up on the mountains
to see the rich man's share;
in search of youthful fountains,
instead, I found you there.

I've crawled across the scalding sands
to see if war was fair;
in search of other peaceful lands,
instead, I found you there.

I've dived into the valleys low
to see if men could care;
in search of missing souls I know,
instead, I found you there.

I've made my way through jungles deep
to see my body wear;
in search of peace for when I sleep,
instead, I found you there.

I've known two worlds: One in my mind,
the other through my stare;
in search of things I'd never find,
instead, I found you there.

I finally understand this life
and feel my sick heart tear;
in the blinded search to end my strife—
Lord, You were always there.

Are We There Yet?

Holding to a steady pace,
from the back seat came a voice.
In belief that life was one long race
and fate, a simple choice.

"Are we there yet?" was his main concern,
as he twisted in his seat.
And I felt the sorrow he would learn
for the trials he had to meet.

"A few more miles...a little while,"
though I knew the trip was long.
But in the mirror beamed a smile,
for my word could not be wrong.

So we talked and laughed, we shared the ride,
and in time he took the wheel.
Through the years we traveled side-by-side
to think, to hope and feel.

Then I turned to him, my tired voice,
"Are we there yet?" was my plea.
He grinned and said, "That's God's own choice."
For at last, my boy could see.

In the End

Standing on the threshold of death,
a lifetime of memories sweeps me away.
My weary mind rewinds every second
and my heart is filled with peace.
I can't seem to recall the material objects
which I once believed had brought me joy.
The cars, the houses, the money—
like grains of blowing sand,
they have sifted through my fingers.
As vivid as the moments we shared,
I only see the faces of those I loved.
I hear the laughter, even cherish the tears.
Like counting sheep, the beautiful smiles of
family and friends appear before me.
But I am tired and it is time to rest.

Awakening above my own wretched body,
my spirit hovers in complete bliss.
There is a sad echo of those who mourn,
but still, I must smile—
for the only thing that ever mattered was love.
As a blessing, I have known that love,
both in giving and receiving
and my life's work is done.

Now, it is time to go to my Father,
but looking back one last time,
I will take all of that love to Him.
As it was in the beginning,
in the end, there is only love.

More than Our Share

out of ghettos, comes the truth
from paupers sent to save
the world from all its evils
which makes each man a slave;
a slave to what he longs for
to all that's bought and sold
lifetimes spent amassing wealth
collecting jewels and gold

forgetting what he came for
his brothers bent in need
searching for some kindness
at least a gentle deed
but wealth is tough to part with
compassion's just as rare
some say, "God didn't give enough."
He did, but we don't share.

Everything

Into the night I cast a wish
that my life, I might share,
and when I least expected love,
you answered every prayer.

I found my heart inside your eyes,
my future—in your smile
and from the day I took your hand
I've cherished every mile.

This path shall lead us to the end
through sun and freezing rain.
Without conditions, I am here
in joy and every pain.

Our love is proof that dreams come true,
I vow in life and death:
That all I am I give to you
with each and every breath.

From the darkness came a light
that only God could bring,
for you are not just who I love…
to me, you're everything.

Learning to Let Go

Before the time of memories,
a teddy bear in tow.
Faith took the first of many steps
when Dad said, "Now let go."

The school bus pulled up right on time,
its strangers in a row.
As Mom sobbed, "I'll be waiting"
and sweaty palms let go.

A tassel hanging from a cap,
the future tied in bows.
The speaker claimed, "To change the world,
the past…we should let go."

A broken heart, a shattered dream
with nothing left to show.
Yet hearts and dreams forget the pain,
but first they must let go.

The rest is taught as life is lived
and those who choose to grow:
Learn hate and spite consume the souls
of those who can't let go.

And as we take our final step
within this world we know:
The hand of God is reaching,
you've learned…

     now

        just

           let

               go.

In Before the Dark

I begged and pleaded, "Let me go. I swear, I won't go far."
He said, "It hurts to watch you grow…
be in before the dark."

I headed out, this stubborn child, a world away from home.
He held my hand through every mile,
not once I walked alone.

I laughed and loved and worked and played,
ignoring every clock,
but heard those words each time I prayed…
"be in before the dark."

I braved the winds and blinding snow, but also felt the sun.
For sixty years of joy and pain,
I stayed out on the run.

Then on it came, the first street light—
yet still came as a shock.
As Father called me from the night…
"be in before the dark."

All is Borrowed

From early days of tutelage,
a child insists, "That's mine!"
Though selfish in its learning,
the truth appears in time.

Possessions are an irony,
belonging to no one.
Material objects, even wealth,
their purpose is for fun.

Some say the earth is ours to keep,
and she keeps us, even so.
You can't sell the rains, or buy the sun,
four winds choose where they'll blow.

As if time was for the taking,
yet sifting through our hands.
To be passed on to the living,
Life's hour glass of sand.

What your eyes behold is borrowed,
not one thing shall you own.
So use it while you have the chance—
even death is just a loan.

The Stranger

A stranger walks up to my door,
in search of warmth and kindness.
Society warns throw the lock
and turn away in blindness.

Peering out the peep hole
at a face from distant dreams.
The eyes look so familiar,
sincere, or so it seems.

Throwing caution to the wind,
the door is opened wide.
Yet, staring back into my eyes,
through my heart he steps inside.

No pleasantries are spoken,
but a smile which has been stored.
A peace then overtakes me,
this stranger is the Lord.

Unity

There is a moth that flutters in the stomach,
searching for that light of love
for which it is so desperately attracted.
Once discovered,
a greater gift cannot be found.
Alas, two hearts beat to the rhythm of one,
beginning life's unpredictable waltz.
Together, taking the hand of the Lord,
they shall be led.
Forever placing each other before themselves,
their spirits glide across a ray of sunlight.
At times, the rain drowns out that gentle harmony,
causing one to stumble, the other fall.
Yet with understanding and simple forgiveness,
the music never stops.
Throughout the song, constant joy proves unrealistic,
but whether each step is smooth or awkward,
complete unity is all they will ever need.
As partners, their unconditional love
shall dance into eternity...

The Only Escape

There is an evil force which pulls at me
and though I don't want to go, my tired mind gives in.
The tunnel of depression is dark and I see no end.
Carrying a tremendous weight upon my shoulders,
I only wish to rest, perhaps sleep forever,
but the fear of staying makes me forge ahead.
I sense that there are others in the tunnel,
but a vicious loneliness tears at my soul.
Each step is agonizing, as I go nowhere.
Finally collapsing onto a cold floor,
I wonder if anyone even knows I am lost;
if anyone knows how to pull me out.
While one last tear tumbles down my twisted face,
a tormenting fear wells up inside of me.
I have reached despair, perhaps for me—the end.
Yet my exhausted spirit shutters to think...
What if it's one more step?

In the blink of a blinded eye, the smallest ray of light
penetrates the blackness that consumes me.
Cautiously, I stand and slowly walk to the light.
With every step, the light's intensity increases and I run.
The brightness warms my face and, for the first time,
I can smile.

Reaching the end of the tunnel, I look back.
Although it is a pain which will linger in my memory,
the brutal maze has finally been conquered.
The answer was simple,
and with me throughout the entire journey:
Hope had always been the only escape.

Happiness

Happiness is found within
before it smiles, awake.
And each shall be entitled,
but not at another's sake.

Always strive to be much more,
but content with what you get.
Everybody wants their share,
though greed leads to regret.

The secret is not found in wealth,
nor success or even fame.
It comes from being truthful.
It's the picture, not the frame.

You may find it in a charity,
or the kind words to a friend.
Discovered in deep poverty,
while for some it's at their end.

Happiness is up to you,
God blessed your every prayer.
But if you find it, let it go—
it's only meant to share.

I Need You

I need you in the morning
when the sun begins anew.
As the birds sing toward the heavens
and the world is fresh with dew.
A youth is filled with mystery,
with much that could go wrong.
I must take a true companion
for I sense the trip is long.

I need you in the afternoon
when the sun has reached its goal.
As the leaves turn different colors
in a world that still seems whole.
A life which has no limits,
brings a joy that knows no pride.
But if I cannot share it,
in the shadows it will hide.

I need you in the evening
when the sun goes down to sleep.
As the rains and winds beat senseless
a world that's forced to weep.
The years have brought both smiles and tears,
through it all, my best I tried.
Yet the outcomes never mattered much,
for You were with me by my side.

Team Effort

For every heartache,
there is a gentle word of compassion.
Each tragedy,
a smile of understanding.
For every tear,
there is a shoulder to accept it.
Each whimper,
the embrace of love.
For every obstacle,
there are the whispers of encouragement.
Each stumble,
a strong, bracing hand.
For every goal,
there are the silent screams of inspiration.
Each triumph,
the applause of those who remained in the shadows,
worrying, hoping and seeing it through.
For everyone is an individual,
yet inevitably, no one is ever alone.
Life is a team effort.

Imprints of Love

It is the spirit that endures, and not the flesh.
Since that is so, how can there be an end?
Throughout our lives, the caring souls of others
will touch us in many permanent ways.
Whether it is merely a compassionate word,
a simple act of kindness or a gentle embrace,
each pure gesture of love
becomes imprinted upon our hearts forever.
Inevitably, as each soul departs from the earth,
those many imprints of love are left behind.
It is through the magnetic spirit
that every person continues to live;
mother living in daughter,
daughter in son—
generously passed down
from one generation to the next,
each soul is touched by many they have never known.
Nobody truly dies.
Our spirits just live within the hearts of others.
So the next time you gaze into a mirror,
peer deeply into your own eyes.
You will see the reflection
of those who have long been gone,
eternally imprinted by love.

Forgiven

From the first day I remember,
it began with one mistake.
Yet feeling truly sorry
in the morning, I'd awake.
My mother would forget it,
as my daddy would forgive.
It would prove to be life's lesson
for as long as I should live.

From the morning of my son's birth
to the day he'd leave the nest.
With a constant need for patience,
for my memory he would test.
As he stumbled toward the answers
and wrestled with the truth,
I would witness all his failings;
a reflection of my youth.

From the last night I would draw a breath
and call this world my home,
I would pray for my own pardon
as my soul at times did roam.
Then kneeling right before the Lord
to bask within His smile.
Yes, the answer was forgiveness—
I had known it all the while.

One True Judgment

Opinions are entitled
to all who shall express,
but when they turn to judgments,
this world becomes a mess.

During times of hardship,
true characters prevail,
yet humans suffer weakness,
at times, we all shall fail.

Gaze into the mirror
and peer into your eyes,
we judge ourselves too harshly,
it comes as no surprise.

But if we grant the Lord respect,
to do what He has said,
there is but one true judgment
for the living and the dead.

Fields of Granite

I stroll through fields of granite
amongst the dear deceased,
sleeping six feet under,
yet to freedom they're released.

No longer in their bodies,
the shells in which they dwelled.
Soaring high above the pain
from this earth, a living hell.

A row of stones, a list of names
of those who did depart.
For some it was a last good-bye,
while for many just the start.

It's like the Lord's own garden,
with His Word, as He had sown.
To reap who had been faithful
for a peace that is unknown.

The rain drowns out the mourning,
while the sun dries all the tears.
For them, it seems like seconds,
but for me, it has been years.

I stroll through fields of granite
and a truth invades my head.
There's a presence of the spirit,
not a memory of the dead.

Ice Cream Cone

Minimum wage and all out of luck,
in sofa cushions, some change was stuck.
Enough to buy one ice cream cone—
we shared it on the long walk home.

And on the trip, the questions flew,
"Why just one cone? And why not two?"
So looking deep within his eyes,
I chose the truth, no need for lies.

Explaining that while life was tough,
with just one cone, we had enough.
He shook his head, took one last taste,
then gave it back and wiped his face.

The pride I felt to watch him share,
at four years old, he didn't care.
As long as we had time to play,
for him it was a perfect day.

For all the dreams that I had built,
to watch them fall, I'd felt the guilt.
But being poor was not a crime
for on my son I'd spent my time.

The Tool Box

I recall the box, I was just a kid
when my dad said, "Here's your tools."
The shock I felt to crack the lid
and discover just one rule.

There were no hammers, nor even screws,
but in the top drawer sat respect.
"It's for walking in another's shoes,
so their hearts you won't neglect."

Instead of pliers, or rusty nails,
in the next drawer sat respect.
"It's to understand when others fail,
so their names you will protect."

Not one wrench, nor a jagged saw
to the bottom just respect.
"All you need, you'll find in any drawer,
so this world you might affect."

I carried that box throughout my days
and this truth I cannot hide.
At times, I'd give away those tools
just to find them locked inside.

The Loss of Death

Death had found me waiting
too eager for his taste.
No kicks, no screams—not one complaint,
for him, it seemed a waste.

He tossed me back into the world
where life held all the fear,
then shook his head in disbelief
to see me wipe a tear.

For me, it seemed so simple,
why Death could bring no sting:
For on a cross, the blood of life
was shed by one true king.

Yet he'll be back, a guarantee—
but from him I'll not hide.
And though Death thinks I'll be afraid,
I know he's just a guide.

Into the promiseland I'll run,
I await that finest hour.
Because of one king's sacrifice,
Death lost all his power.

Home

Beyond the stars,
though my mind's eye struggles to remember,
there is a place from whence my soul had come.
My heart, however, trickles distant glimpses...
In this glorious existence:
There is no use for sunlight, nor food,
for any substance needed to flourish
comes from unconditional love.
It is where time holds no captives,
as the past, present and future converge into one,
and one brief moment is like a billion years.
All the secrets of the universe are revealed
and there is no want for anything.
Dark shadows do not exist in this dimension,
for peace and serenity replace all pain.
All that is beautiful and kind and righteous dwells here
sent into the world we know—
if only to experience and appreciate all that was created.
My spirit, merely one part of the whole,
has spent the gift of life stumbling around
in search of answers.
Yet, perhaps the truth is not meant to be discovered
but simply remembered...
Each of us remembering who we are,
the love that sent us to illuminate this world
and the home that awaits our return.

Two Angels

The Lord sent down two angels,
a sort-of sacred test.
With broken wings, but hearts of gold,
the world must do the rest.

Confined to tiny wheelchairs,
they search for good, not bad,
but face a million burning stares
from eyes that look so sad.

Into the clouds, their spirits soar
in the midst of those with health
and cause the wise to stand in awe
to ask the worth of wealth.

Drowned out moans that, "Life is hard,"
with laughter, oh so sweet,
they teach the precious will of God,
keeping others on their feet.

The Lord sent down two angels,
an example of His love.
With knowing eyes and gentle smiles,
a glimpse of life above.

One Favor

You've lived within my sweetest dreams,
your voice, your smell, your stare—
and on the night an angel spoke,
I found you standing there.

Kindness, truth, a hint of love
betrayed within a glance.
As if I was still dreaming,
I prayed for just one chance.

For all the struggles I endured,
the wrongs I tried to right—
I always knew I'd walk through hell
to find you on that night.

And there you were, just smiling
aglow with peace and love;
the answer to my every wish
I'd sent to God above.

I dare not ask for one more thing
from God—He's done His part.
From you I beg one favor:
Please take care of my heart.

Frozen

Heading down a crooked path of white stained-glass,
a bitter soul stood hunched against the cold.
On winds, the truth came howling in an Arctic blast;
for you, I think it best this tale be told:

Though this eve was one of beauty,
with its trees all dipped in white,
and like folds within a sheet the earth stretched long.
The hum of one man's breathing, hot enough
for ice to melt
betrayed a hatred for all men within his song.

Though the moon showed off its halo,
cast upon the drifting snow,
and a million wishes sparkled in the frost.
Just behind this stranger's curtain, sat the pride,
the greed and rage
and in turn, the precious moments that were lost.

Though the world lay still with wonder,
with a wolves' bite in the air,
and it seemed it might all crack and take no more.
Instead, the mercury kept slipping,
enough to cease one blinded heart,
or perhaps enough to coax that heart to thaw.

Bend

Bend to the truth
and feel with your heart.
Through love and compassion,
you may do your part.

Bend not your ear,
to the words of a fool.
But strive to forgive,
as if pain were a jewel.

Bend to the wind
and sway with the trees.
Accept all that's happened
for a life blessed with ease.

Bend at the knees
and search for His grace,
for the world shall be heaven,
a most glorious place.

Ten Lifetimes More

Lord,
I want to say, "Remember when..."
to those who won't ignore,
the last words of a dying man,
I ask—one minute more.

I have to say, "I'll miss you,"
to strangers by the score.
Now that my life on earth is through,
I plead—two minutes more.

I failed to say, "I'm sorry,"
to those I've treated poor.
And since I'm in no hurry,
I beg—five minutes more.

And the simple words, "I love you,"
to those I still adore:
For they must know my heart was true,
I need ten lifetimes more.

Broken Shell

Twinkling eyes of liquid blue,
a chiseled face, with jet black hair.
The perfect shell possessed by few,
adored by those who stare.

The chance to meet a mate of choice,
a gift from God above.
Instead, with mischief in his voice,
he chooses lust, not love.

But time decides to play its game
with weather and disease,
and mirrors never look the same,
as youth becomes the tease.

In a wink, it's faded—gone to hide,
but the toughest search will tell:
Is there any beauty left inside,
or only a broken shell?

A Walk in the Clouds

I walked amongst the clouds today
and then I took a seat
to try to understand the world
that spun beneath my feet.

It was the grandest picture
my eyes had ever seen.
I couldn't make out colors,
except for blue and green.

And yet, I could see people;
a whole race on the run.
To tell the truth, from where I sat
they clearly moved as one.

With fear, they searched for answers
they thought were on the ground,
and though they spoke in different tongues
they made the sweetest sound.

They had the wrong perspective
with no way they could know:
There are no individuals—
just parts of a whole.

And so I made a wish for them
that someday they would see:
Only when they really love
is when they're really free.

I'll dance amongst the stars tonight,
while others search in vain.
For just above their point of view,
there's no such thing as pain.

Crossroads of Love

Two roads began at separate points
in a time called, "long ago."
To wonder then where they would lead
was a fate for God to know.

Each guided children down their paths
of goodness, hope and love.
With nothing but the light that shone
from heaven up above.

The obstacles, the bumps and turns
which stood in both their ways
were merely just a set of tests
that led to better days.

The rains would pass, the winds subside
and with their labor done,
two roads would stop and take the time
to watch the setting sun.

But God had other plans in mind:
Their trips had just begun.
Two roads began at separate points,
but now those roads are one.

Wishes

We wish for you, upon your birth,
to touch the stars, explore the earth.
While doing so, the best of health
for there is not a greater wealth.

We wish for you, as you shall grow,
all the wisdom one could know.
And here's a secret: As you live,
to find true joy you need to give.

We wish for you when times are tough,
to trust your faith shall be enough.
For dreams live on were there is hope
and in the truth, you'll learn to cope.

We wish for you, as years roll past,
respect, compassion—that they last.
So others may return the same
and honor shall protect your name.

We wish for you, above all things,
the love that friends and family bring;
That God shall bless each breath you take…
a difference will your own life make.

In the Silence

A creaky chair, the beat of heart
a moment caught alone.
In the silence—long-forgotten
the memory aches for home.

A gentle wind, the waltzing trees
a quilt of soothing rain.
In the silence—wisdom captured
the lessons learned from pain.

A twinkling star, the winter's moon
a rhythmic, steamy breath.
In the silence—depths of wonder
the truths that lead to death.

A simple prayer, the searching mind
a test of man's own will.
In the silence—every answer
the need to just be still.

The Greatest Teachers

My children have taught me...

that trust is sealed before the first step
and real understanding does not require words;
that a baby's breath and angels' wings make
the same sound,
and bonds forged on sleepless nights are eternal.

My children have taught me...

that the greatest wonders are found within
the smallest moments;
and the grip of a tiny hand slips away much too fast;
that the word "proud" can inspire unimaginable feats,
while the word "disappointed" can scar the soul.

My children have taught me...

that doing something means so much less
than being there,
as one day at the park is more valuable than
ten visits to the toy store;
that laughter is contagious and can destroy all worries,
and Santa Claus is alive and well—
all that's needed is faith.

My children have taught me…

that the most powerful prayers are made up of
the simplest words,
humbled, grateful and spoken from the heart;
and that for most ailments, the best medicine is a kiss
or a hug for someone who wouldn't dream of asking.

My children have taught me…

that friends can be made with no more than a smile
and real blessings are found amongst family and friends;
that the future promises magic and wonder,
and that dreams must be chased until each one
comes true.

Death

So we meet again…
the first time was in the desert
all those years ago.
I was young and scared.
You were cruel and taunting.
I thought I was alone then.
I was too young to know.

So now you're back…
but I'm no longer afraid.
I've grown in my faith,
learning that we're never alone.
And you—you're the one
who takes us home,
you're the eternal chauffer.

So let's ride, I've got people waiting.

Wishing Life Away

If I can just get through this day...
beyond the traffic and morning news,
the in-box and bagged lunch,
the homework and evening prayer.

If I can just get to the weekend...
beyond the drop offs and pick ups,
the cooking and 'time-outs,'
the popcorn and reality shows.

If I can just get past this month...
beyond the weekend chores,
the emails and calls to return,
the worry over unpaid bills.

If I can just get to the new year...
beyond the hustle and constant chaos,
the deadlines and deliverables,
the same old, same old.

If I can just get through this day...

In My Dreams

In my dreams, I've seen a place
where smiles are worn on every face;
where not a child is ever sick
but love flows freely, sweet and thick.

In my dreams, I've felt a peace
where pain and fear and doubt have ceased;
where past transgressions are erased,
leaving mercy in their place.

In my dreams, I've tasted hope
with no more reason—just to cope;
where sunrise happens all day long
and desperate cries have turned to song.

In my dreams, I've smelled success
worn by those who once had less.
Instead, they chose to give it all,
selfless service is their call.

In my dreams, the angels sing—
not with voices, but with wings.
I realize now I'm not alone
for heaven is our blessed home.

I Am With You

for my friend, Amber Nicole Cowen

Feel my peace—I am home now
where there is no darkness
and worries are no more than a faded memory.
I am with family, those who love me
And—I am still with you.

Just listen—I am the beat of your heart
and in every breath you take.
You will find me in your laughter
and in the silence when you cuddle on the couch.
I am on the wind; amongst the patter of rain.
Listen closely and there I am—with you.

Just look—I am a morning's ray of light
and the first snowflake of winter.
You will find me in the shadows of a dance
and in the smiles of those who love you.
I am amongst the stars, on the sparkling sea.
Look carefully and there I am—with you.

Just feel—I am the embrace of an old friend
and in the handshake of some stranger you've helped.
You will find me in those moments of pure joy
and in the sun's warm hands upon your face.

I am the flutter of an angel's wings—perfect, blessed.

Feel my peace—I am with you

still

always

Home to You

so many yesterdays
searching, fumbling
steps taken in the darkness
wondering if I'd ever find my way;
every road block, obstacle
each hardship leading me to you
no mistakes
just tests that needed to be passed
to where I belonged…

to home…

to You

Soaring

I close my eyes and take three deep breaths…
I am soaring above the dense green forest,
high above the chirping birds and dancing butterflies;
amidst a baby blanket of drifting clouds
and the majestic flight of a bald eagle.
The air is warm and scented in pine.
I hover above a rolling emerald pasture
and land before a doe and her stumbling fawn.
And I witness the true spirit of innocence.

I close my eyes and take three deep breaths…
I am soaring above a powdered-sugar desert,
high above the ruby red ridges and starving cacti;
amidst the haunting calls of circling scavengers,
their deadly song echoing through deep, dark canyons.
The air is stifling but filled with hope.
Toward the vast horizon, I chase the setting sun
and unknown colors that melt across the great canvas.
And I discover the entrance to heaven.

I close my eyes and take three deep breaths…
I am soaring above a chiseled mountain range,
high above the sentinel oaks and dripping peaks;
amongst the dens of black bear and bobcats,
and sapphire lakes that reflect a million twinkling stars.
The air is cool but comfortable.

I float on my back for a millennium,
gazing into the universe and all its miracles.
And I understand the meaning of peace.

I close my eyes and take three deep breaths…
I am soaring above the crowded city streets,
high above the sounds and smells of humanity;
between the giant structures of fluorescent lights
and a thousand black-tarred rooftops.
The air is dank and dirty.
I slowly descend into a tree-lined park
to find a homeless man seated upon a bench.
And I peer into the eyes of God.

About the Author

Steven Manchester is the author of the #1 bestsellers *Twelve Months, The Rockin' Chair, Pressed Pennies* and *Gooseberry Island*; the national bestsellers, *Ashes, The Changing Season* and *Three Shoeboxes*; the multi-award winning novels, *Bread Bags & Bullies: Surviving the '80s* and *Goodnight Brian,* and the beloved holiday audio podcast, *The Thursday Night Club*. His work has appeared on NBC's Today Show, CBS's The Early Show, CNN's American Morning and BET's Nightly News. Three of Steven's short stories were selected "101 Best" for Chicken Soup for the Soul series. He is a multi-produced playwright, as well as the winner of the 2017 Los Angeles Book Festival and the 2018 New York Book Festival. When not spending time with his beautiful wife, Paula, or their four children, this Massachusetts author is promoting his works or writing. Visit: www.StevenManchester.com

facebook.com/AuthorStevenManchester

twitter.com/authorSteveM

Made in the USA
Middletown, DE
16 March 2021

35370151R00035